How to Stop Being Defensive in Your Marriage

A Step-by-Step Guide to Heal Old Wounds, Stop Feeling Attacked, Build Healthy Relationship, and Resolve Conflicts Through Effective Communication

SANDY MATHIAS

Copyright © 2024 by Sandy Mathias

All rights reserved. No part of this book may be reproduced or transmitted in any form or by any means, electronic or mechanical, including photocopying, recording, or by any information storage and retrieval system, without permission in writing from the publisher.

The information provided in this book is designed to provide helpful information on the subjects discussed. The author and publisher disclaim any liability or loss in connection with the use or misuse of this information. It is recommended that readers consult with appropriate professionals before taking any actions based on the information in this book.

TABLE OF CONTENTS

CHAPTER 1 9
WHY WE GET DEFENSIVE IN MARRIAGE 9
Understanding the Underlying Causes 10

The High Cost of Defensiveness: How It Damages Your Relationship 12

The Power of Vulnerability 16

CHAPTER 2 21
RECOGNIZING THE CYCLE OF DEFENSIVENESS 21
Identifying Your Triggers: What Makes You Shut Down? 22

The Cycle of Defensiveness: A Recipe for Conflict 26

Taking Responsibility for Your Reactions 29

CHAPTER 3 33
CULTIVATING EMPATHY AND UNDERSTANDING ... 33
Hearing Your Partner Beyond Their Words 34

Accepting Your Partner for who they are 37

Overcoming the Pitfall of Criticism and Blame 41

Finding Peace: Letting Go of Grudges 46

CHAPTER 4 51

EFFECTIVE CONFLICT RESOLUTION STRATEGIES .. 51

The Power of Forgiveness 52

From Fighting to Finding Solution 57

What Makes Relationships Healthy? 61

Establishing a Healthy Boundary 68

Conclusion 71

INTRODUCTION

Why We Build Walls Instead of Bridges in Our Marriages

Remember that first year of marriage? Everything felt new, exciting, and full of possibility. You couldn't wait to spend every moment with your partner, sharing dreams, hopes, and vulnerabilities. Communication felt effortless, like a secret language only the two of you understood.

Fast forward a few years (or maybe even a few months, life can be surprising). Arguments erupt like sudden storms, leaving behind a trail of hurt feelings and unspoken resentments. Conversations feel laced with landmines, where one wrong word can trigger an explosion. You find yourselves withdrawing, building walls instead of bridges, and wondering where that initial spark went.

Maybe you recognize this scenario. Maybe you and your spouse are locked in this frustrating cycle of defensiveness and conflict. Believe me, you're not the only one. It's a common pitfall in many marriages, a place where love gets shrouded in frustration and connection gets lost in the crossfire.

The truth is, defensiveness is a natural human response. When we feel attacked, judged, or misunderstood, our instinct is to build a shield to protect ourselves. In the safe space of a marriage, however, this protective armor can become a barrier to intimacy and understanding.

But here's the good news: this cycle doesn't have to define your relationship. You can break free from the constant battles and rebuild a marriage based on trust, communication, and empathy.

This book, "How to Stop Being Defensive in Your Marriage," isn't here to point fingers or assign blame. It's a friendly guide, a hand reaching out to help you navigate the often-turbulent waters of communication. It's about understanding why defensiveness creeps in, how it fuels conflict, and most importantly, what you can do to break free from its grip.

We'll probe into the hidden triggers that make you shut down and look at ways to identify those triggers in yourself and your partner. We'll learn how to cultivate empathy and truly hear each other's perspectives, even when you disagree. You'll discover the power of "I" statements and how to own your feelings without resorting to blame.

But communication is just one piece of the puzzle. We'll also look into strategies for effective conflict resolution, learning to shift the focus from winning and losing to finding solutions together. You'll discover the importance of forgiveness and letting go of old hurts, paving the way for a more peaceful and connected relationship.

Ultimately, this book is about building a stronger, more resilient marriage. It's about creating a safe space where you can both be vulnerable, express your needs openly, and work through challenges as a team. We'll discover ways to maintain open communication and healthy habits over time, keeping the spark alive and the connection strong.

I know that this won't be easy. It takes effort, commitment, and a willingness to be open and honest with yourself and your partner. But the rewards are immeasurable. Imagine a marriage where open communication replaces defensiveness, where arguments become opportunities for growth, and where a deep sense of love and respect forms the foundation of your relationship.

This book is going to help you to reach that destination. You are going to rediscover the joy and connection of your early days, build a marriage that can weather any storm, and create a love story that grows more beautiful with each passing year.

So, are you ready to take down those walls and build bridges of understanding? Let's begin.

CHAPTER 1

WHY WE GET DEFENSIVE IN MARRIAGE

UNDERSTANDING THE UNDERLYING CAUSES

Have you ever found yourself in a heated argument with your spouse, feeling like you're under attack, even when the topic seems trivial? It's a scenario many of us have experienced, and it often leads to defensiveness. But why do we get defensive in our marriages?

Common Reasons for Defensiveness

At the heart of defensiveness in marriage lie a multitude of emotions and vulnerabilities. One of the primary reasons is fear. We fear being misunderstood, rejected, or criticized by our partner. Dr. John Gottman, a renowned psychologist and relationship expert, explains, "Defensiveness is typically a response to feeling attacked, criticized, or blamed." When we perceive a threat to our self-worth or our relationship, our natural instinct is to protect ourselves, sometimes by putting up walls or deflecting blame.

Another common trigger for defensiveness is insecurity. We may feel insecure about our abilities, our worthiness as a partner, or the stability of our relationship. These insecurities can manifest as defensiveness when our partner's words or actions trigger our fears of inadequacy or abandonment. Dr. Sue Johnson, a clinical psychologist and founder of Emotionally Focused Therapy (EFT), emphasizes the role of attachment needs in triggering defensive responses in relationships.

Past experiences also play a significant role in shaping our defensive behaviors. Childhood experiences, previous relationships, and even cultural influences can contribute to our emotional responses in marriage. For example, if we grew up in an environment where criticism was common or where we felt the need to constantly prove ourselves, we may carry those defense mechanisms into our adult relationships. Dr. Harriet Lerner, a psychologist and author specializing in relationships, explains, "Our past experiences shape the lens through which we view our current relationships. If we felt criticized or belittled in the past, we may be more prone to defensiveness in our marriage."

Self-Reflection Exercise

Take a moment to reflect on your own defensive tendencies in your marriage. Think about a recent disagreement or argument with your spouse. What were the underlying emotions driving your defensiveness? Were you feeling fearful, insecure, or perhaps reminded of past experiences? Consider how these emotions may have influenced your reactions during the conflict.

Now, think about recurring patterns in your defensive behavior. Do certain topics or situations tend to trigger your defensiveness more than others? Are there specific words or actions from your partner that consistently evoke a defensive response from you? Identifying these triggers can help you gain insight into your defensive tendencies and pave the way for healthier communication in your marriage.

THE HIGH COST OF DEFENSIVENESS: HOW IT DAMAGES YOUR RELATIONSHIP

Defensiveness in marriage can exact a heavy toll on the health and longevity of a relationship. Its repercussions ripple through various aspects of a partnership, corroding communication, eroding trust, and fracturing emotional bonds. At its core, defensiveness serves as a barrier to understanding and resolution, creating a chasm between partners that widens with each defensive response.

In the realm of communication, defensiveness acts as a formidable obstacle, obstructing the flow of meaningful dialogue between spouses. When one partner becomes defensive, they often deflect blame or criticism, shutting down avenues for constructive conversation. This breakdown in communication can lead to a cycle of misinterpretation and frustration, where genuine concerns are drowned out by the clamor of defensiveness. For instance, consider a scenario where one partner raises a concern about financial decisions, only to be met with defensiveness and excuses. Instead of addressing the root of the issue, the defensive response hampers any chance of finding a mutually beneficial solution, leaving both partners feeling unheard and disconnected.

Moreover, defensiveness corrodes the foundation of trust within a relationship, sowing seeds of doubt and suspicion. When a partner consistently responds defensively to feedback or criticism, it undermines the trust that is essential for a healthy partnership. Over time, this erosion of trust can breed resentment and distance, as each defensive reaction chips away at the fragile bonds of trust that hold a relationship together. Consider the case of a partner who becomes defensive when questioned about their whereabouts or activities. Rather than fostering transparency and honesty, this defensive response fosters doubt and insecurity, poisoning the wellspring of trust between partners.

Another point is, defensiveness exacts a profound toll on the emotional connection between spouses, diminishing intimacy and closeness. When one partner consistently responds defensively, it creates a climate of emotional distance and disconnection. Instead of feeling emotionally supported and understood, partners may feel isolated and alienated, unable to express their true thoughts and feelings for fear of eliciting a defensive response. This erosion of emotional connection can lead to feelings of loneliness and dissatisfaction, as partners struggle to bridge the gap created by defensiveness. For instance, imagine a partner who shares their vulnerabilities and insecurities, only to be met with defensiveness and dismissal. Rather than fostering empathy and closeness, this defensive response erects barriers to emotional intimacy, leaving both partners feeling emotionally adrift.

In real-life scenarios, the damaging effects of defensiveness are readily apparent, as couples grapple with conflict and discord fueled by defensive responses. Consider a couple who constantly bickers over household chores, each partner becoming increasingly defensive when confronted with the other's grievances. Instead of addressing the underlying issues and finding common ground, defensiveness exacerbates tensions, transforming minor disagreements into major rifts. Over time, the accumulation of unresolved conflicts and defensive responses can poison the well of goodwill between partners, leading to resentment and disillusionment.

Similarly, in the face of significant challenges or setbacks, defensiveness can further strain a relationship, impeding efforts to navigate adversity together. Imagine a couple facing financial difficulties, with one partner becoming defensive and evasive when asked about their spending habits. Rather than working together to find solutions and support each other through tough times, defensiveness breeds resentment and blame, driving a wedge between partners.

THE POWER OF VULNERABILITY

In marriage, being open and honest with each other is like glue that holds everything together. Some people think being open makes you weak, but it's actually a brave thing to do. When couples are open with each other, they build trust and understanding, making their relationship stronger.

Think of vulnerability as showing your true self to your partner. It's like saying, "This is me, with all my flaws and fears." Sharing your worries and insecurities with your partner creates a safe space where you both can be yourselves without being judged. This trust and acceptance bring you closer together emotionally.

Being vulnerable isn't just about sharing deep secrets. It's also about being open in everyday situations. For example, admitting when you're feeling stressed or asking for help when you need it shows vulnerability. It lets your partner know they can rely on you and vice versa.

When couples are open with each other, they can tackle problems together. Instead of blaming each other during tough times, they work as a team to find solutions. This teamwork strengthens their bond and helps them grow closer.

In the end, vulnerability isn't about winning or losing. It's about being brave enough to be yourself, even when you're not sure how your partner will react. When you are open and vulnerable, you can build a relationship filled with trust, love, and understanding.

But why is vulnerability so powerful in marriage?

Building Trust Through Openness

Trust is the cornerstone of any successful relationship, and vulnerability plays a crucial role in its cultivation. When partners are open and honest with each other, it creates a foundation of trust that allows them to feel secure and supported in their relationship. Dr. John Gottman, a leading researcher in the field of marital stability, emphasizes the importance of trust in fostering intimacy, stating, "Trust is the glue of life. It's the most essential ingredient in effective communication. It's the foundational principle that holds all relationships."

By being vulnerable with each other, couples demonstrate a willingness to be transparent and authentic, which fosters trust and strengthens their emotional connection. When partners feel they can rely on each other to be open and honest, it deepens their bond and allows them to navigate challenges and conflicts with greater ease.

Fostering Intimacy Through Authenticity

In addition to building trust, vulnerability also fosters intimacy within a marriage. When partners are willing to share their deepest thoughts, feelings, and vulnerabilities, it creates opportunities for deeper emotional connection and understanding. Dr. Harville Hendrix, a pioneer in couples therapy, emphasizes the importance of emotional intimacy in sustaining a fulfilling relationship, stating, "The quality of our relationships determines the quality of our lives."

By embracing vulnerability and allowing themselves to be fully known and accepted by their partner, couples can experience a profound sense of emotional closeness and connection. When partners feel they can be themselves without fear of judgment or rejection, it creates a space where they can truly bond and grow together.

Challenging Misconceptions About Vulnerability

Despite its importance in fostering connection and intimacy, vulnerability is often misunderstood and misrepresented in our society. Many people equate vulnerability with weakness, viewing it as a liability rather than a strength. However, vulnerability is anything but weak—it requires immense courage to expose our fears, insecurities, and innermost thoughts to another person.

Dr. Brené Brown, a renowned researcher and author on vulnerability, eloquently captures its importance, stating, "Vulnerability is the birthplace of love, belonging, joy, courage, empathy, and creativity. It is the source of hope, empathy, accountability, and authenticity." In essence, vulnerability is the cornerstone of authentic connection, allowing partners to show up as their genuine selves and be truly seen and accepted by their spouse.

So how can couples cultivate vulnerability in their own marriage? Here are some practical steps they can take to embrace openness and authenticity:

1. Practice Active Listening: Take the time to listen to your partner without judgment or interruption. Create a safe space where they feel heard and understood.

2. Share Your Feelings: Be open and honest with your partner about your thoughts, feelings, and concerns. Don't be afraid to express vulnerability and show your true self.

3. Be Empathetic: Put yourself in your partner's shoes and try to understand their perspective. Show empathy and compassion for their experiences and emotions.

4. Encourage Open Communication: Foster a culture of open communication in your relationship, where both partners feel comfortable expressing themselves freely.

CHAPTER 2

RECOGNIZING THE CYCLE OF DEFENSIVENESS

IDENTIFYING YOUR TRIGGERS: WHAT MAKES YOU SHUT DOWN?

Sometimes in our marriage, our triggers—those emotional buttons that, when pressed, cause us to react defensively—can have a profound impact on the health and happiness of our relationship. When we understand these triggers, it can help us in fostering open communication and resolving conflicts in a constructive manner.

Common Defensive Behaviors

1. Stonewalling: I want you to picture this: You're in the midst of a heated argument with your spouse, emotions running high, and suddenly, they go silent. No words, no eye contact—just a cold, impenetrable wall. This is stonewalling, a defensive behavior characterized by shutting down communication entirely. When one partner stonewalls, it effectively puts a halt to any meaningful dialogue, leaving the other feeling unheard and frustrated. Dr. John Gottman, describes stonewalling as one of the "Four Horsemen of the Apocalypse," indicating its destructive potential in marriages.

2. Blaming: Another common defensive behavior is blaming. When faced with criticism or conflict, some individuals instinctively deflect responsibility onto their partner, shifting the focus away from themselves. For example, a spouse who, when confronted about forgetting an important event, immediately blames their partner for not reminding them. This blame-shifting not only avoids accountability but also escalates tensions and impedes resolution.

3. Minimizing: Minimizing involves downplaying the significance of a partner's concerns or feelings, dismissing them as unimportant or exaggerated. For instance, imagine expressing frustration to your spouse about their habit of leaving dirty dishes in the sink, only to be met with a casual wave of the hand and a dismissive, "It's not a big deal." This minimizing response invalidates your feelings and undermines the importance of open communication in addressing relationship issues.

Impact on Communication and Conflict Resolution

These defensive behaviors—stonewalling, blaming, and minimizing—can have profound consequences on communication and conflict resolution in marriage. Rather than fostering understanding and resolution, they serve to shut down dialogue and perpetuate discord.

When one partner stonewalls during a conflict, it creates a barrier to communication, leaving the other partner feeling shut out and frustrated. Without the opportunity to express their thoughts and feelings, resentment can build, further straining the relationship. Stonewalling also prevents the resolution of underlying issues, as important concerns go unaddressed and unresolved.

Similarly, blaming shifts the focus away from finding solutions to the problem at hand, instead fostering defensiveness and finger-pointing. This blame game only serves to escalate tensions and erode trust between partners, making it difficult to find common ground and move forward together.

Minimizing further exacerbates communication breakdowns by invalidating a partner's feelings and concerns. When one partner dismisses the other's emotions as insignificant, it creates a sense of disconnection and invalidation, hindering the development of emotional intimacy and trust.

Exploring Past Experiences

Our defensive behaviors in marriage are often influenced by past experiences, such as a difficult childhood or previous failed relationships. For example, someone who grew up in a household where conflict was avoided may resort to stonewalling as a means of self-preservation. Similarly, individuals who experienced criticism or blame in past relationships may be more prone to defensive behaviors like blaming or minimizing in their current marriage.

Self-Reflection Questions

To help you identify your personal triggers and defensive behaviors in marriage, consider the following questions for self-reflection:

1. What topics typically make me feel defensive in conversations with my spouse?

2. How do I react when I feel criticized or attacked during an argument? Do I tend to shut down, blame my partner, or minimize their concerns?

3. What body language do I use when I'm starting to shut down? Do I avoid eye contact, cross my arms defensively, or withdraw physically from the conversation?

4. Are there any patterns in my defensive behaviors that I've noticed over time? How do these patterns impact communication and conflict resolution in my marriage?

5. How have past experiences, such as my upbringing or previous relationships, influenced my defensive tendencies in marriage?

By reflecting on these questions honestly and openly, you can gain valuable insight into your triggers and defensive behaviors, paving the way for greater self-awareness and growth in your relationship.

THE CYCLE OF DEFENSIVENESS: A RECIPE FOR CONFLICT

When defensiveness takes hold in a marriage, it triggers a predictable cycle that keeps the conflict simmering just below the surface. Here's how it unfolds:

1. A Criticism or Complaint: The cycle usually starts with a criticism or a complaint. It could be anything from "You never take out the trash" to "I feel neglected because you're always working."

2. Defensive Reaction: Instead of acknowledging the underlying issue, one partner becomes defensive. This could manifest as justifying their behavior ("I work long

hours to support us!"), minimizing the issue ("It's not that big of a deal"), deflecting blame ("You never compliment me!"), or even getting angry.

3. Escalation: This defensive reaction triggers a counter-reaction from the other partner. Feeling unheard and frustrated, they may escalate by using sarcasm, raising their voice, or resorting to personal attacks.

4. Emotional Withdrawal or Stonewalling: Often, faced with escalation, one partner shuts down emotionally. They may become withdrawn, silent, or refuse to engage further. This "stonewalling" behavior creates emotional distance and leaves the other partner feeling even more frustrated.

5. Feeling Hurt and Unloved: Both partners are left feeling hurt and unloved. The person who initiated the conversation feels dismissed and unheard, while the defensive partner feels attacked and misunderstood.

6. Repeat: This cycle can become a frustrating loop. With each repetition, the underlying issue remains unaddressed, and the resentment grows, making future communication even more challenging.

The Dance of Blame and Counter-Blame

One of the most destructive aspects of defensiveness is the "dance of blame and counter-blame." In this scenario, the focus shifts away from understanding the root cause of the conflict to a competition of who's right and who's wrong. Each partner becomes entrenched in their own perspective, unwilling to consider the other's point of view. This constant blame game fosters negativity, erodes trust, and makes finding a solution nearly impossible.

Here's how the dance of blame hinders progress:

Prevents Empathy: When blame takes center stage, there's no room for empathy. Partners become too focused on defending themselves to understand how their actions might have impacted the other person.

Focuses on the Past: The dance of blame keeps the couple reliving past hurts and grievances. Instead of moving forward, they get stuck in a cycle of negativity.

Hinders Open Communication: Blame shuts down open communication. Partners become hesitant to express themselves honestly for fear of being judged or attacked.

TAKING RESPONSIBILITY FOR YOUR REACTIONS

In every of human relationships, conflicts are inevitable. Whether it's a minor disagreement or a major dispute, how we react in these moments can either perpetuate the cycle of conflict or lead us toward resolution and growth. One of the most powerful tools in breaking the cycle of defensiveness and fostering healthier conversations is taking responsibility for our own reactions.

When faced with criticism, disagreement, or perceived attacks, our instinctual response often veers towards defensiveness. This reaction stems from a primal urge to protect ourselves, our beliefs, and our egos. However, what often goes unnoticed is the role we play in escalating conflicts, even if we believe our partner initiated it.

Imagine a downward spiral: one partner voices a concern or disagreement, which triggers defensiveness in the other. This defensiveness, instead of resolving the issue, intensifies the conflict, leading to further criticism, more defensiveness, and ultimately, disconnection. Each defensive reaction fuels the other, creating a loop that's difficult to break.

Breaking this pattern begins with acknowledging our own role in it. It's tempting to blame our partner for triggering our defensive reactions, but true growth happens when we recognize that we have control over how we respond. By taking ownership of our reactions, we empower ourselves to interrupt the cycle and steer the conversation towards a more constructive path.

Choosing Conscious Communication

Conscious communication involves being mindful of our thoughts, emotions, and reactions in the heat of the moment. Instead of defaulting to automatic defensiveness, we pause, take a breath, and respond with intention. This shift from reactive to responsive communication is important in fostering healthy conversations.

When we consciously choose our words and tone, we create space for empathy, understanding, and resolution. Rather than escalating the conflict, we invite our partner to engage in a dialogue based on mutual respect and collaboration. This doesn't mean suppressing our emotions or avoiding difficult topics; it means expressing ourselves in a way that promotes connection rather than division.

Journal Exercise

Journaling can be a powerful tool for self-reflection and exploration. Here are some prompts to help you examine your defensive behavior and past experiences:

1. Reflect on a recent conflict with your partner. What triggered your defensive reaction? How did you contribute to the escalation of the conflict?

2. Think back to your childhood or past relationships. Were there instances where you learned to be defensive as a coping mechanism? How does this affect your current interactions?

3. Consider a time when you successfully navigated a difficult conversation without resorting to defensiveness. What strategies did you use? How can you apply them in future conflicts?

4. Imagine your ideal way of responding to criticism or disagreement. What steps can you take to align your reactions with this ideal?

1. I lied about a speeding ticket to my wife, and then got defensive and said "it wasn't that big of a deal". I didn't immediately take the full fault.
2. In the past I have had a tendency to blame others or circumstances for my faults.
3. Taking a deep breath, thinking about how my actions impacted my partner. Realizing I was in the wrong.
4. My ideal way would be to respond constructively, and use it as an opportunity to get better.

CHAPTER 3

CULTIVATING EMPATHY AND UNDERSTANDING

HEARING YOUR PARTNER BEYOND THEIR WORDS

In a marriage, communication isn't just about talking. It's about truly understanding each other. But sometimes, we get caught up in our own thoughts and miss out on what our partner is really trying to say. That's where active listening comes in.

Think about a time when your partner came home looking tired and frustrated. They started talking about their day, but you could tell there was more going on beneath the surface. Active listening means paying attention not just to the words, but also to the feelings behind them. It's about showing that you care about what your partner is going through.

In marriage, active listening is like a superpower. When you really listen to your partner, you show them that their thoughts and feelings matter to you. This creates a safe space for honest communication and strengthens your bond.

Active listening also helps you to understand your partner's emotions, even when they don't say them out loud. Sometimes, the real message isn't in the words, but in the feelings behind them. By tuning in to these emotions, you deepen your connection and intimacy with your partner.

In simple terms, active listening is all about empathy—putting yourself in your partner's shoes and really understanding where they're coming from. When you listen with empathy, you build trust and respect in your marriage, which are the foundations of a strong relationship.

Actionable Plans: Do's and Don'ts for Active Listening

To become a better listener, there are some things you should do and some things you should avoid:

Do:

1. Be Present: Focus on your partner when they're talking to you. Put away distractions and give them your full attention.

2. Show Empathy: Let your partner know that you understand how they're feeling. Use phrases like "I can see why you feel that way" to show that you're listening.

3. Ask Open-Ended Questions: Encourage your partner to share more by asking questions that can't be answered with a simple yes or no.

4. Paraphrase and Reflect: Repeat back what your partner has said in your own words to make sure you've understood correctly. Reflect their emotions back to them to show that you're listening.

5. Validate Their Feelings: Even if you don't agree with your partner, let them know that you respect their feelings.

Don't:

1. Interrupt: Wait until your partner has finished speaking before you respond. Interrupting can make them feel like you're not really listening.

2. Offer Unsolicited Advice: Sometimes, your partner just needs someone to listen, not to solve their problems. Hold back on giving advice unless they ask for it.

3. Get Defensive: Try to stay calm and open-minded, even if you don't like what your partner is saying. Getting defensive can shut down communication.

4. Invalidating Their Feelings: Avoid dismissing your partner's emotions, even if you don't think they're justified. Everyone has a right to their feelings.

5. Make Assumptions: Don't jump to conclusions about what your partner is thinking or feeling. Instead, ask them directly to clarify.

By following these simple do's and don'ts, you can become a better listener and strengthen your marriage. Remember, active listening isn't just about hearing the words—it's about understanding the person behind them. So, next time your partner speaks, take a moment to really listen. You might be surprised by what you hear.

ACCEPTING YOUR PARTNER FOR WHO THEY ARE

Have you ever noticed how certain couples effortlessly emanate love and affection? Indeed, it's a beautiful phenomenon with a solid foundation. These couples have embraced each other wholly, fostering deeper intimacy and a more vibrant love connection.

When we fail to accept our partners entirely—with all their quirks and habits—we convey that they're inadequate. Who wants to feel that, especially in matters of the heart?

Simply put, when acceptance wanes, so does the flow of love.

Even porcupines grasp this concept! Despite their protective quills, they know to retract them and embrace closeness.

If porcupines can accept their loved ones, quirks included, shouldn't we?

The following are key practices to foster acceptance:

Avoid Trying to Change Your Loved One

Attempting to change someone implies non-acceptance. Many of us persistently try to alter our partners' traits or behaviors, to no avail.

I, too, faced this struggle. My husband desired orderliness, while I accumulated clutter. He attempted persuasion and coercion, but it only strained our relationship.

Realizing his powerlessness, he accepted me as I was. This acceptance strengthened our bond, and surprisingly, eased his own anxieties.

Simply put, acceptance begins with ourselves.

Lower Your Expectations

High expectations breed disappointment and resentment. I learned this the hard way, as my expectations stifled our relationships.

As love progresses, expectations tend to rise. But expecting too much signals non-acceptance.

Consider whether your needs are solely your partner's responsibility. Often, they're not.

Respect Your Partner's Choices

Everyone has their own path. We may wish the best for our loved ones, but we can't dictate their choices.

Acceptance involves acknowledging their autonomy, even when it challenges our views.

Acceptance Is a Choice

Ultimately, accepting our partners is a decision we must make. We can't change them, but we can control our own actions and attitudes.

Choose acceptance, and watch the love flourish!

Allow me to share my story for your further reflection

Acceptance, as I've come to realize, is not just a practice but a profound shift in perspective. It's about embracing the entirety of your partner—their strengths, weaknesses, and everything in between.

In my own journey towards acceptance, I've encountered moments of resistance and doubt. There were times when I questioned whether accepting my husband's quirks meant compromising my own values or desires.

Yet, as I delved deeper, I uncovered a truth that transcended these concerns.

Acceptance isn't about surrendering your identity or sacrificing your needs. Rather, it's about recognizing the beauty in our differences and finding harmony amidst the chaos of everyday life.

For me, acceptance meant acknowledging that my husband's penchant for order didn't invalidate my love for spontaneity. It meant finding joy in the messiness of our shared experiences and learning to appreciate the unique perspective he brought to our relationship.

Moreover, acceptance paved the way for growth and self-discovery. By releasing the need to control or change my husband, I freed myself from the burden of unrealistic expectations. I began to see our relationship not as a project to be perfected but as a journey of mutual understanding and growth.

Of course, acceptance isn't always easy. It requires patience, empathy, and a willingness to let go of preconceived notions. Yet, the rewards far outweigh the challenges.

Today, as I look back on our journey, I'm grateful for the lessons that acceptance has taught me. It has transformed our relationship from one of discord to one of harmony and connection. And in embracing my husband fully, flaws and all, I've discovered a love that is truly unconditional.

So, to anyone embarking on their own journey of acceptance, I offer this advice: Trust in the power of acceptance to transform not only your relationship but also yourself. Embrace the imperfections, cherish the differences, and above all, love fiercely and unapologetically. For in the end, it is love that truly conquers all.

OVERCOMING THE PITFALL OF CRITICISM AND BLAME

If you're anything like me, you aspire to embody your best self in your primary relationship. You aim to express love, kindness, and support, and to witness the rewards these qualities bring to your love life. However, certain patterns of interaction often obstruct these aspirations, leaving you feeling inadequate and ashamed.

Like many, I was raised in an environment steeped in criticism and blame. Despite my intellectual rebellion against this behavior, its influence penetrated deeply within me.

As the initial euphoria of love wore off in my more serious relationships, criticism and blame emerged, leaving me wracked with guilt and disappointed in myself. This detrimental habit invariably created distance in my relationships.

It's no surprise that this habit ranks as a primary reason relationships falter. Not only does it inflict pain upon the recipient, but it also corrodes the perpetrator's confidence and integrity, hindering the free flow of love.

Reflecting on my first marriage, I recognize that this ingrained and destructive habit corroded the foundation of our love. My subtle forms of blame and criticism, often masked as requests, permeated our interactions. Like unbridled weeds, they gradually suffocated our joy.

Criticism and blame manifest in both overt and subtle ways. While explicit expressions are evident in our chosen words, subtler forms often inflict more damage due to their imperceptibility.

Since a significant portion of communication is non-verbal, it's crucial to scrutinize how we convey blame and criticism without words.

Some subtle manifestations include:

Tone of voice: Uttering requests with a tone dripping with blame or implying incompetence.

Sounds: Emitting sighs or groans that convey exasperation.

Body language: Rolling eyes or giving cold glances, gestures that speak volumes.

Subtle demands for improvement: While ostensibly constructive, they can harbor undertones of criticism.

In my present partnership, I vowed to chart a different course. I embraced my partner without reservations or complaints, fostering years of authentic, tolerant, and loving interactions. I took pride in seemingly transcending my past shortcomings.

However, we encountered a rough patch. A stressful year filled with the demands of a newborn, coupled with the challenges of building a home, placed immense strain on me. Amidst this turmoil, my old habit of blame and criticism resurfaced, seemingly beyond my control.

I found myself subtly belittling my partner, masking criticism as innocent remarks. Despite my remorse, I felt powerless to halt this destructive pattern. Consequently, my partner grew defensive, and I sank deeper into self-loathing, fearing I might jeopardize the most precious aspect of my life.

It was a wake-up call. I took time to recuperate and regain balance, affording me the clarity to confront my shortcomings.

The insights I gleaned have largely liberated me from this harmful pattern, and I share them with you, along with practical tips to nurture and enrich the love in your life:

1. Nurture Self-Compassion:

Avoid directing blame inward. Instead, cultivate kindness and curiosity towards yourself. Understand that criticism and blame stem from a misguided attempt to safeguard oneself and the relationship, albeit through ineffective means. Cultivating self-compassion lays the groundwork for a more authentic and loving relationship.

2. Embrace Responsibility:

Acknowledging and taking responsibility for your missteps is pivotal to overcoming them. Whether in the heat of the moment or later, owning up to your errors, and offering a sincere apology can soften your partner's defenses and foster understanding.

3. Recognize Fear's Role:

Beneath every expression of blame or criticism lies fear. Uncover the underlying fears driving your negative emotions. This self-awareness promotes curiosity, compassion, and integrity, fostering a deeper connection with your authentic self.

4. Harness the Power of Movement:

When gripped by blame or criticism, engage in physical movement to release tension and shift your perspective. Whether through dance, walking, or relaxation techniques, movement can restore equilibrium and reconnect you with your innate kindness and goodness.

5. Cultivate Appreciation:

Counteract negativity bias by consciously seeking moments of appreciation. Redirect your attention towards your partner's positive qualities, fostering gratitude and deepening your bond.

Through this journey of self-discovery and growth, I've emerged with renewed confidence in my ability to nurture love in my partnership. By acknowledging and transcending our shortcomings, we pave the way for a relationship grounded in authenticity, kindness, and unwavering love.

Just as a gardener tends to her garden, diligently uprooting weeds and nurturing blossoms, so too can we cultivate and nurture love in our lives. With patience, compassion, and commitment, we can transform our relationships into vibrant sanctuaries of love and acceptance.

FINDING PEACE: LETTING GO OF GRUDGES

Are you tired of it?

You keep arguing, feeling more and more angry.

You know explaining won't help, so you stop talking.

But the argument still bothers you...

That's how it was in my marriage.

At first, we argued all the time. After each fight, I couldn't stop thinking about what went wrong, what hurt me, and what I wanted my partner to do differently.

Days would pass without us speaking, and I'd feel more and more angry inside.

After a while, I'd reach out, even though I was still mad.

But how long could this go on?

All those fights and grudges were hurting our marriage. They were pushing us apart, making us forget why we loved each other in the first place.

Then I asked myself, "Where are we going? Are we going to let these grudges ruin our marriage?"

After thinking about it, I realized our fights were usually about small things, not big issues. They weren't about who we really were as people.

One of our big problems was chores. I wanted my partner to help without me asking, but he didn't think to do it unless I said something.

I'd get so mad waiting for him to help that by the time I finished the chores, I'd snap at him for no reason.

It wasn't good for us.

So we decided to make a change. We decided to focus on our marriage first and let go of the little things, most of the time.

Holding grudges is like poison.

Deep down, you know you shouldn't let them bother you. They steal your happiness and make you feel sick inside.

Is it worth it to stay mad?

No way!

Protect Your Happiness

Sometimes we hold grudges against our partners, friends, or family. We're all imperfect, and living with other people can be hard.

But we can choose to save our relationships, at least some of the time.

If you're at a point where you're deciding whether to stay in the relationship or leave, try thinking about these seven things after you've cooled down:

1. Think About Winning:

When you were arguing, you probably wanted to win. But now that you're calmer, do you still care about winning? Is this issue really worth damaging your relationship over?

2. Consider How Important the Argument Is:

When you're angry, it's hard to think clearly. But after you calm down, ask yourself if this argument really matters. In my marriage, I realized most of our fights were about small things we could fix by talking to each other.

3. Remember Every Relationship Has Problems:

No relationship is perfect. There will always be arguments. So think about whether you want to be alone just because of one fight.

4. Ask Yourself If You're Really Winning:

Keeping a grudge might make you feel like you won, but what are you giving up? It's not good for your peace of mind. You're hurting yourself more than anyone else.

5. Try Forgiving:

Forgiving someone can be hard, but it can also make you feel free. I've found that forgiving people, even for small things, helps me be a happier person.

6. Look at the Big Picture:

Think about all the good times you've had with this person. Is this fight really worth ending your relationship over? Can you talk about it and find a solution together?

7. Decide if You Want to Ruin Your Relationship:

Letting go of a grudge doesn't mean giving up. It means choosing your happiness over being mad. Do you want to keep being angry, or do you want to let it go and move on?

Choose Peace Over Anger

Grudges only make you feel worse.

Do you really want to keep feeling this way?

Letting go of grudges can help you feel happier and healthier.

So choose to let go of the anger and focus on what really matters—your peace of mind and your relationships.

CHAPTER 4

EFFECTIVE CONFLICT RESOLUTION STRATEGIES

THE POWER OF FORGIVENESS

It's normal to feel angry when we think we've been wronged. Anger is a natural response to tough situations, especially when we feel our rights have been violated or our safety is at risk. Recognizing and accepting our anger is a crucial part of understanding our emotions.

While it's okay to feel angry, holding onto that anger for too long can be harmful. The saying "Carry a grudge" illustrates how heavy and burdensome resentment can be. When we hold onto anger, we use up energy to keep that negative feeling alive, which only makes us suffer more and adds to our stress. This burden becomes even heavier when the person who hurt us has apologized and tried to make things right. That's when forgiveness becomes important.

Forgiveness isn't easy. It takes a lot of strength and bravery. While seeking revenge might feel like a way to make the other person understand our pain, it usually just makes things worse. Revenge might give us a momentary feeling of satisfaction, but in the end, it damages our relationships and leaves emotional scars.

Forgiveness is hard for a few reasons. First, the desire for revenge feels more natural – it's a way to get back at the person who hurt us. Giving up that desire can feel like we're letting them off the hook. Also, seeking revenge gives us a clear outcome – seeing the other person suffer. Forgiveness, on the other hand, might leave us with unresolved feelings at first because it doesn't give us that immediate satisfaction.

Despite its challenges, forgiveness has many benefits. It's a brave choice that can improve our mental health, our relationships, and our sense of well-being. Forgiveness frees us from the weight of anger and allows us to move forward without carrying around resentment. Even though forgiveness might not bring instant results, focusing on the positive impact it has on us and our relationships can motivate us to choose forgiveness over holding onto anger.

In relationships, saying sorry and forgiving each other are powerful ways to show love. It takes strength to apologize sincerely, and forgiving someone shows even more strength.

Forgiving isn't easy. When someone hurts us or breaks our trust, it feels like they've taken something important from us – like our trust and our belief that everything will be okay. It's easier to stay angry than to admit that we can be hurt. But everyone goes through this, even the people we care about the most. They can hurt us deeply because they know us so well.

But, deep down, love means accepting the parts that scare us. Forgiving is like a higher form of love—it's not just for others, but it's also for ourselves. We can only truly forgive when our hearts are full of love. Choosing to forgive is not just about them deserving it; it's about us deserving inner peace. Forgiveness is a big part of finding real peace.

Unfortunately, there's no magic fix for the common problems that come up in relationships. So, the next best thing is getting good at dealing with issues, fights, and annoyances, and maybe coming out even stronger. Forgiveness is one way to do this. In relationships, forgiving means changing how we feel, think, and act towards our partners. It's about letting go of bad feelings (like holding onto grudges, giving up revenge, and getting rid of anger) and bringing in good feelings (like understanding and kindness) towards our partner.

But forgiving doesn't mean we're saying everything is okay, letting things slide, or forgetting what happened (especially if it's something really bad). So, forgiveness happens even if the other person doesn't really deserve it.

Basically, being able to forgive is a deep way of showing love in a relationship. Forgiveness can make your relationship happier, and stronger during tough times, and just work better overall. Forgiving your partner can also be really good for your own health and happiness. Even if they don't say sorry, forgiveness is still possible.

However, forgiving takes time. Even if we wish it could be an easy choice that happens right away, it's usually more complicated. Forgiving is like a slow process where you carefully remove a poison that could hurt both you and your relationship. The good part is that forgiveness is possible, and it can make a big difference for you and your relationship. Of course, forgiveness alone isn't enough for a great relationship, just like one piece can't make a clock tick. But in the workings of your relationship, forgiveness is a big piece, and you might find that forgiving your partner brings great rewards for everyone involved.

Focus on the Big Picture: During conflicts, prioritize the larger goal of strengthening your relationship rather than winning arguments. Instead of seeking to prove yourself right, aim for mutual understanding and collaborative problem-solving. While winning a small argument may bring temporary satisfaction, it doesn't contribute positively to the long-term health of your relationship.

Empathize: Put yourself in your partner's shoes and try to understand their perspective. Consider their feelings and experiences, as well as the detrimental effects of anger or distance on both of you and your relationship. Acknowledge your own emotions while striving to express them in a way that fosters constructive dialogue and mutual support.

Release Grudges: Rather than keeping a mental tally of your partner's mistakes, choose to address grievances calmly when both of you are in a peaceful state. Encourage open communication and active listening, allowing space for both perspectives to be heard and understood. Holding onto grudges not only damages the relationship but also burdens your own well-being.

Combat Negative Thoughts: Challenge the critical inner voice that undermines your happiness and relationship satisfaction. Disregard thoughts that promote self-sabotage or vindictiveness, opting instead for actions aligned with your shared relationship goals and values.

Explore Intimacy Concerns: Reflect on how personal fears regarding intimacy may influence your behavior in the relationship. Recognize and address these concerns to facilitate more positive interactions and deepen emotional connection.

Separate Past Family Issues: Be mindful of how past family experiences might shape your perceptions and behaviors in your current relationship. Avoid projecting negative dynamics onto your partner and assess whether your actions align with your present values and aspirations.

FROM FIGHTING TO FINDING SOLUTION

Ever experienced a minor disagreement with your partner that escalated into a full-blown conflict? It's a scenario many of us can relate to.

In such moments, it's easy to become irritable and adopt an ostrich-like approach, burying our heads and ignoring our partner's perspective. We may even justify our grumpiness or anger, entering a "war" mentality where winning becomes paramount.

In this state, we construct metaphorical trenches, arm ourselves, and barely listen to our partner's viewpoint, fixating solely on hearing those coveted words: "I'm sorry, you're right."

Perhaps you've found yourself in this situation before; I know I have. It used to occur frequently whenever my partner and I disagreed, and truth be told, I still struggle with it today.

It became a habitual response rooted in pride; I was unwilling to admit fault, even when it harmed our relationship.

I've come to realize that such reactions are detrimental to love and care within a relationship. During arguments, pride often blinds us, overshadowing our ability to prioritize the health of our connection.

Every time pride fuels a conflict, it creates a fracture in the relationship. Initially inconspicuous, these fractures gradually widen until they become irreparable, akin to a crack in a car window left unattended.

Is preserving one's pride truly worth jeopardizing a relationship? For me, the answer is a resounding no.

I value the success, fulfillment, and love within my relationship above all else. Consequently, I've endeavored to switch off the "pride switch" during conflicts.

Admittedly, this is no easy feat. The resistance to yield during heated moments is strong. However, I've discovered practical strategies to respond more effectively in such situations, fostering productive conflict resolution instead of destructive outcomes.

1. Pause and Choose Your Response:

When faced with a conflict, it's crucial to resist the urge to react impulsively. Instead, take a moment to pause and assess the situation objectively. Consider the potential outcomes of different responses. Will responding with anger or defensiveness escalate the conflict, or will it foster understanding and resolution?

2. Ask Reflective Questions:

Reflective questioning involves introspection about the consequences of your actions and words. Before engaging in a conflict, ask yourself whether your chosen reaction aligns with your values and goals for the relationship. Will you feel proud of your response later, knowing that it contributed positively to the connection with your partner? This introspective approach encourages mindful communication and helps prevent impulsive reactions driven by ego or frustration.

3. Acknowledge the Other's Feelings:

Conflict often arises from a failure to recognize and validate each other's emotions. Break the cycle of defensiveness by actively listening to your partner's perspective and acknowledging their feelings without immediately offering counterarguments or justifications. Simply acknowledging their emotions can diffuse tension and create an atmosphere conducive to constructive dialogue.

4. Avoid Rhetorical Questions:

Rhetorical questions, particularly accusatory ones, can exacerbate conflicts by placing blame or provoking defensiveness. Instead of framing your concerns as interrogations, communicate them directly and assertively while maintaining a respectful tone. Clearly express your needs and concerns without resorting to rhetorical tactics that undermine productive communication.

5. Apologize Freely:

Apologizing is a powerful tool for diffusing conflicts and repairing relational rifts. It's essential to recognize that offering an apology is not a sign of weakness but rather a gesture of humility and empathy. When you realize that your actions or words have caused harm or misunderstanding, don't hesitate to apologize sincerely. By taking responsibility for your behavior and expressing remorse, you demonstrate your commitment to the relationship's well-being and pave the way for reconciliation and mutual growth.

WHAT MAKES RELATIONSHIPS HEALTHY?

When seeking a healthy relationship, it's important to focus on what truly matters in a partner and in the relationship itself. While some may chase after a magical "spark" or believe they've found "the one," it's equally crucial to consider if the relationship is genuinely good for you. Before finding happiness with someone else, understanding how to nurture a healthy relationship is key.

Rather than solely concentrating on your partner's qualities or what they do for you, take a step back and examine the relationship as a whole and how you both interact within it. What makes this relationship stand out? What draws you and your partner together?

Visualize the happiness and satisfaction you bring into each other's lives. Imagine feeling completely loved and content with someone. How does that make you feel, and why?

Think about what sets this potential relationship apart. While you may not have an immediate answer, it likely embodies many, if not all, of the qualities that define a healthy relationship.

Regardless of how long you've been together, whether it's been a short week or a decade, you can develop important relationship skills. To build and sustain a great relationship, it's essential to consciously practice positive behaviors and effective communication. As these habits become routine in your connection with your partner, you can look forward to a wonderful, loving, and enduring relationship that you truly deserve.

Love Yourself: Embrace the idea that "You attract what you are." This means the energy you project and the way you treat yourself and others directly impact the relationships you form. Cultivating positivity, passion, and kindness towards yourself and others naturally draws similar individuals into your life. Learning to love yourself isn't always easy. It requires identifying and overcoming negative beliefs while building self-confidence. However, it's a crucial initial step towards fostering healthy relationships.

Set High Standards: Strive to uphold high standards for yourself to cultivate a fulfilling relationship. If you lack effort or set low expectations, the connection with your partner may stagnate and deteriorate over time. Reflect on your desires from the relationship. What emotional and physical qualities do you seek in an ideal partner? Ensure that the standards you set for your partner align with those you hold for yourself. Remember, you play an active role in the relationship, and the treatment you expect from your partner should mirror how you treat them.

Meet Your Partner's Needs: Prioritize meeting each other's needs in a mutually supportive manner. The more attentive you are to your partner's needs, the stronger your relationship will become. Take the time to understand what your partner requires most—whether it's comfort, security, or feeling valued—and how they prefer those needs to be addressed. It's not merely about awareness but empathizing with their feelings and being present for them. Ask yourself if your partner is your top priority and consider what you're willing to do to nurture the relationship while also finding happiness within it.

Communicate Well: Effective communication is vital for nurturing healthy relationships. Avoid assuming your partner's desires; instead, actively listen to their expressed needs. In a mutually respectful relationship, communication involves considering what you can contribute to your partner's well-being, not solely focusing on your own needs. By understanding and addressing both your needs and your partner's, you can work together to strengthen your bond. Reflect on the lengths you would go to for someone you deeply care about, as meeting important needs fosters happiness, love, passion, and trust.

Grow Together: Embrace challenges and obstacles as opportunities for growth within your relationship. Challenges propel personal and relational development; without them, stagnation may occur. Embrace uncertainty and new experiences as avenues for growth, even if they initially make you feel uncomfortable. Don't allow fear to hinder your personal growth or the progression of your relationship. Instead, view each challenge as a chance to evolve and strengthen your connection with your partner.

Appreciate Differences: Instead of brushing aside or minimizing your differences, embrace them. It's essential to acknowledge and cherish the distinct qualities that both you and your partner bring to the relationship. These differences initially attracted you to each other and should remain cherished aspects of your bond. By valuing each other's uniqueness, you not only enhance the quality of your shared life but also find joy in it.

Be Honest: Honesty forms the bedrock of healthy relationships, including being truthful with yourself. Remaining authentic and self-assured is vital for navigating challenges positively. It's crucial to confront disappointments, pain, and surprises with honesty and bravery. Even in the most loving relationships, moments of sadness can arise. Instead of avoiding issues, confront them with honesty and courage, trusting in your ability to overcome any obstacle alongside your partner.

Reimagine Intimacy: Intimacy encompasses more than physical connection; it also involves the small, everyday gestures—like watching a favorite movie together or preparing your partner's favorite meal unprompted. If establishing a connection feels challenging, persist in your efforts. Sustaining a healthy relationship requires ongoing investment. Share your thoughts and emotions to address problems and prevent resentments from accumulating.

Explore Opposites: A healthy relationship thrives on the balance of contrasting energies. One partner may exhibit certainty and focus, while the other embodies spontaneity and openness. These divergent energies can fuel a profound attraction. Continuously explore these differences to maintain the spark of passion in your relationship.

Match Your Values: Despite being in a healthy relationship, disparities in values and long-term aspirations may arise. A successful partnership leverages these differences as opportunities for growth rather than sources of discord. Reflect on your core values and future aspirations. Are your partner's communication style and goals aligned with yours? While discrepancies in these areas can present challenges, they also have the potential to deepen passion, intimacy, and connection.

Change Your Focus: As you strive for a healthy relationship, maintain clarity and commitment. Your focus directs your energy. Will you dwell on problems, or will you channel your efforts into seeking solutions? Opt for the latter approach, enabling you to effectively address challenges and appreciate how your differences enrich your shared life.

Keep It Going: Having learned the principles of a healthy relationship and established a solid foundation, sustain its strength by setting a positive example and nurturing your loving bond. Remember, you always retain agency, regardless of life's challenges. You can allow pain to inflict harm on yourself and your partner, or you can derive wisdom from adversity and apply those lessons to enhance your life. A healthy relationship demands continual effort, regardless of its duration. Therefore, remain open to new experiences, inject excitement, and ensure your relationship brims with vitality and passion—while never forgetting to savor the journey together.

ESTABLISHING A HEALTHY BOUNDARY

When we hear the term "boundary," it often evokes negative connotations because it implies limitations or restrictions. However, establishing boundaries can significantly benefit your mental well-being.

Growing up, I was accustomed to prioritizing others' needs over my own. This pattern persisted into adulthood, resulting in feelings of exhaustion and emotional depletion. While being a dependable source of support for others is gratifying, it can also be draining, particularly when neglecting my own emotional needs. My tendency to seek approval from others further compounded this struggle.

My difficulty with setting boundaries traces back to my upbringing. I was raised in a tumultuous environment marked by frequent parental conflicts. As a result, I often found myself caught in the crossfire, attempting to mediate without success. I learned to suppress my own emotions to avoid exacerbating tensions, fostering a belief that my needs were inconsequential and that trusting others was perilous.

For a prolonged period, I remained oblivious to the concept of boundaries and how to establish them.

However, with personal growth, I've come to appreciate their significance. Nevertheless, mastering boundary-setting proved challenging. Initially, I attempted to enforce boundaries without explanation, which left me feeling disempowered. Now, I approach boundary-setting with mindfulness and compassion, considering both my own well-being and that of others.

1. *Choose the right time and setting:* This means picking a suitable moment and environment to discuss your boundaries. It's crucial to have the conversation when the other person is calm and receptive. For instance, avoid bringing up sensitive topics during busy or stressful times, like rush hour traffic or right after a hectic day at work.

2. *Show that you care:* Before diving into the topic of boundaries, start the conversation with some small talk or inquiries about the other person's well-being. This helps create a comfortable atmosphere and shows that you value the relationship. Demonstrating care and interest in the other person's feelings can make them more open and receptive to discussing boundaries without feeling attacked or defensive.

3. Be gentle but clear: When addressing the subject of boundaries, approach it with compassion and clarity. Express how you feel and why you need to set boundaries in a gentle and non-confrontational manner. Avoid blaming or accusing the other person, and instead focus on owning your feelings and needs. Clearly communicate what boundaries you need to establish and why they are important for your well-being. Being gentle yet clear helps ensure that your message is understood without causing unnecessary conflict.

4. Stick to your boundaries: Once you've set boundaries, it's essential to uphold them firmly. Don't allow the other person to manipulate or disregard your boundaries. Stay resolute in asserting what you need to maintain your emotional health and respect for yourself. It may be challenging, especially if the other person reacts negatively or tries to push back against your boundaries, but standing firm is crucial for your self-esteem and maintaining healthy relationships.

5. Reassure the person: If the other person reacts negatively to your boundaries, reassure them that your intention is not to reject them or diminish the relationship. Emphasize that setting boundaries is about taking care of yourself and maintaining your well-being. Offer reassurance that you still value the relationship and are committed to finding a balance that respects both parties' needs. Reassuring the other person helps alleviate any fears or insecurities they may have and fosters understanding and respect for your boundaries.

CONCLUSION

Congratulations! You've reached the end of this journey together. Throughout these pages, we've explored the complexities of communication in marriage, delving into the roots of defensiveness and the power of vulnerability. You've learned to identify your triggers, cultivate empathy for your partner, and navigate conflict with newfound skills.

Remember, building a strong and lasting marriage is an ongoing practice. There will be bumps along the road, moments when old patterns resurface. But the tools you've acquired in this book will equip you to face challenges with understanding, respect, and a willingness to grow together.

As you move forward, prioritize open communication. Make time for regular check-ins, nurture intimacy, and keep the spark alive. Remember, a happy marriage takes effort from both partners, but the rewards are immeasurable.

This book wouldn't have been possible without the hope of helping couples build stronger, more fulfilling relationships. If the strategies and insights resonated with you, and you feel empowered to navigate conflict with more empathy and understanding, we'd be incredibly grateful if you could consider leaving a positive review and rating for "How to Stop Being Defensive in Your Marriage" on Amazon.

Your feedback helps us reach more couples seeking to build a love story that endures. We believe in the power of communication and the transformative strength of vulnerability in marriage.

Thank you for embarking on this journey with us. Here's to a lifetime of love, laughter, and connection with your spouse!

Made in the USA
Middletown, DE
15 May 2025

75586501R00042